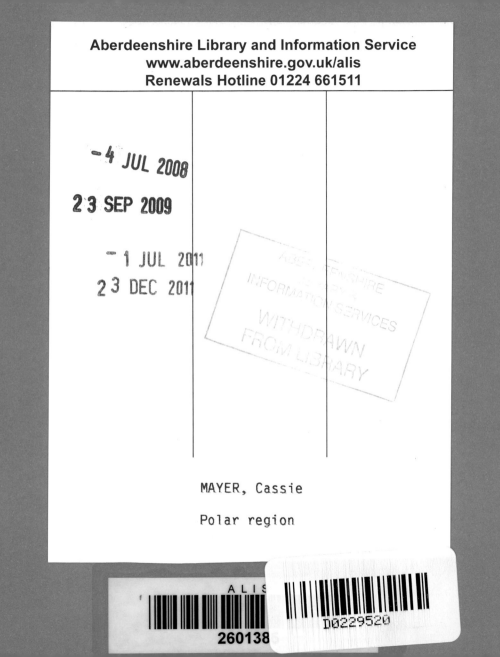

MAYER, Cassie

Polar region

LIVING AND NON-LIVING

Polar Region

Cassie Mayer

Heinemann
LIBRARY

H **www.heinemann.co.uk/library**
Visit our website to find out more information about Heinemann Library books

To order:
☎ Phone 44 (0) 1865 888066
▤ Send a fax to 44 (0) 1865 314091
▢ Visit the Heinemann Bookshop at www.heinemann.co.uk/library to browse our
catalogue and order online.

First published in Great Britain by Heinemann Library,
Halley Court, Jordan Hill, Oxford OX2 8FJ, part of Harcourt
Education. Heinemann is a registered trademark of Harcourt
Education Ltd.

Editorial: Cassie Mayer and Diyan Leake
Design: Kimberly Miracle
Illustration: Mark Beech
Picture research: Erica Martin and Melissa Allison
Production: Duncan Gilbert

Originated by Modern Age
Printed and bound in China by South China
Printing Co. Ltd

ISBN 978 0 431 18460 9
12 11 10 09 08
10 9 8 7 6 5 4 3 2 1

British Library Cataloguing in Publication Data
Mayer, Cassie
  Living and Non-living: Polar Region

A full catalogue record for this book is available from the
British Library.

Acknowledgements
The publishers would like to thank the following for permission
to reproduce photographs: Alamy pp. **5** (Bryan & Cherry
Alexander Photography), **7** (Juniors Bildarchiv), **15** (Bryan &
Cherry Alexander Photography); Bryan & Cherry Alexander
Photography p. **19**; Getty Images pp. **6** (Frank Krahmer), **8**
(Wayne R. Bilenduke), **9** (Paul Nicklen), **11** (Kevin Schafer),
13, **14** (Taxi/John Giustina), **16** (Kim Heacox), **20** (The Image
Bank/Joseph Van Os), **22** (Photodisc Red/Darrell Gulin),
23 (iceberg image: Taxi/John Giustina), **back cover** (Kim
Heacox); Nature Picture Library pp. **10** (Brandon Cole), **12**
(Georgette Douwma), **18** (Pete Oxford), **21** (Pete Oxford)
23 (penguin image: Pete Oxford); Photolibrary pp. **4** (Digital
Vision/Robert Harding), **17** (Index Stock Imagery), **23** (polar
region image: Digital Vision/Robert Harding).

Cover photograph of a polar bear mother and cubs in Norway
reproduced with permission of Getty Images/Photodisc Red
(Darrell Gulin).

Every effort has been made to contact copyright holders of any
material reproduces in this book. Any omissions will be rectified
in subsequent printings if notice is given to the publisher.

Contents

A polar region habitat

A polar region is an area of land.
A polar region is very cold.

A polar region has living things.
A polar region has non-living things.

Polar bear

Is a polar bear a living thing?

Does a polar bear need food? *Yes.*
Does a polar bear need water? *Yes.*

Does a polar bear need air? *Yes*.

Does a polar bear grow? *Yes*.

So a polar bear is a living thing.

Whale

humpback whale

Is a whale a living thing?

Does a whale need food? *Yes.*
Does a whale need water? *Yes.*

Does a whale need air? *Yes.*

Does a whale grow? *Yes.*

So a whale is a living thing.

Iceberg

iceberg

Is an iceberg a living thing?

Does an iceberg need food? *No.*
Does an iceberg need water? *No.*

Does an iceberg need air? *No.*

Does an iceberg grow? *No.*

An iceberg is not a living thing.

Penguin

Is a penguin a living thing?

ice – frozen water

Does a penguin need food? *Yes.*
Does a penguin need water? *Yes.*

Does a penguin need air? *Yes.*

Does a penguin grow? *Yes.*

So a penguin is a living thing.

A polar region is home to many things. A polar region is an important habitat.

Picture glossary

habitat area where plants and animals live

iceberg large piece of floating ice

polar region a habitat that is very cold

Index

Notes for parents and teachers
Before reading
Talk to the children about living and non-living things. Ask them how they would know
if something is living or non-living. Help them to come to some conclusions about the
characteristics of both living and non-living things.

After reading
Show children where the polar regions are on a globe. Talk about icebergs which float
in the Artic and Antarctic oceans. Fill a small bag full of water and freeze it. Then place
the ice lump in a tray of water. Talk about floating and how there is more of the iceberg
below the water than above.
Look at the DVD or read the book *March of the Penguins*. Talk about the environment
where the penguins live.